# LIVING WELL

## Spending Less

## &

## unstuffed

STUDY GUIDE | 8 SESSIONS

# RUTH SOUKUP

with Lori Vanden Bosch

ZONDERVAN®

*Living Well Spending Less & Unstuffed Study Guide*
© 2018 by Ruth Soukup

This title is also available as a Zondervan ebook.

Requests for information should be addressed to:
Zondervan, *3900 Sparks Dr. SE, Grand Rapids, Michigan 49546*

ISBN 978-0-310-09244-5

First Printing September 2018 / Printed in the United States of America

# Contents

# Introduction

Do you ever feel like you've spent your life chasing after the good life, only to discover that all the things you thought you wanted haven't made you happy? Have you ever wondered whether a life of contentment is even possible?

Me too.

I know what it's like to want what I can't afford, and I know just how scary it can be to get caught up in a downward spiral of out-of-control spending. How it can consume your life, eat up your time, and destroy your relationships. Early in my marriage, there was constant change. Pretty much the only thing that stayed consistent in my life was the mall. And Amazon.com. And Target. Pottery Barn. Williams-Sonoma. Gymboree. I filled our life with stuff, but it never filled the void.

But God had a plan for even a broken shopaholic like me, and I discovered that sometimes grace is shaped like a coupon. I hit bottom in my own journey and learned a totally different way to think about money and possessions . . . and discovered true happiness along the way.

These days, I'm passionate about saving money, not because I think I've got this personal finance thing all figured out—believe me, I don't! I still make financial mistakes every single day. I'm months behind on my filing system. I struggle to stay within my budget. I neglect balancing my checkbook. I spend money on things I shouldn't. And every single month I procrastinate paying my bills.

I'm passionate about saving money—and about helping others to do the same—not because I have all the answers, but because I have learned that money—whether too much of it or too little—permeates every area, every single facet, of our lives. Ultimately, how we spend our money is a direct reflection of what's in our hearts.

Are you ready to tackle your own financial missteps and begin a journey toward a life rich in the things that matter most? If so, join me as we unpack the secrets of the good life. Because while I may not always have it all together, I have faith in the God who does.

Together we'll learn to shift our priorities toward treasures that last. And when we do, we'll find a life rich in faith, family, friends, and creativity—and a budget that balances and a home and life that are unstuffed. The good life is waiting for you. Are you ready to find it?

*—Ruth*

# How to Use This Guide

Welcome to the *Living Well Spending Less/Unstuffed* video study! We hope you will enjoy this small-group experience. As part of your time together, you will be using this study guide, which includes video teaching notes, group discussion questions, and between-sessions personal studies to help you reflect on and apply the material to your life during the week.

To get the most out of this study, you should commit both to the group study *and* the personal study on your own time. Both the group discussions and the personal studies will help you process and apply the content of Ruth Soukup's video message. Committing to the group, attending each session, and coming prepared to share what you learned in your personal study will help you build trust and rapport with the other members. However, if you are unable to finish a personal study, you should still attend the next group study. You are still wanted and welcome at the group even if you don't have any "homework" done.

Your small group is a place for sharing stories, learning about God, and building intimacy and friendship. For this reason, keep everything your group shares confidential. Be thoughtful and honest in your responses, and listen carefully and compassionately to the opinions and experiences of others. This will foster a rewarding sense of community in your group and create a place where people can heal, be challenged, and grow spiritually.

In between your group time, continue to learn and grow by doing the "Personal

Study" section of your study guide. In this section you will do some Bible study to help you reflect on deeper spiritual and emotional issues, but at times you will be asked to live out what you've learned in practical ways. Take notes and come ready to share how you did; you will be surprised how much you can learn from one another's real-life experiences!

You are also encouraged to read *Living Well Spending Less* and *Unstuffed*, the books on which this curriculum is based. They will provide you with a wealth of inspirational stories, tips, and motivating tricks to help you manage not only your home but also your heart as well. See the "Book Time" box for the chapters in the book that correspond to the material your group discussed that week.

As you go through this study, watch for what God is saying to you about living well and spending less. Ask him to show you what you are doing well and where you need to change. Ask him for his help in unstuffing all the things that hold you back. Then share your stories and experiences with your group. There is no better way to deepen your relationship with God and to grow in his grace than to listen, learn, and love him alongside your fellow believers.

---

**Note:** If you are a group leader, there are additional instructions and resources provided in the back of this guide to help you lead your group members through the study.

---

# LIVING WELL
## Spending Less

# What Is the Good Life?

The good life is not about what we have
but about embracing who we are in Christ.

## Opening Reflection

The insatiable desire for more is a disease that permeates every fiber of our being. Overconsumption and unchecked indulgence in anything—whether it's food, alcohol, drugs, or possessions—will eventually destroy us. It doesn't matter if we're barely squeaking by or we have more than we know what to do with—though most of us fall somewhere between those two extremes. Discovering the good life is not just about learning to spend less but about actually changing the desires of our heart, shifting our priorities from wanting and hoping for the best of everything in this world to deeply longing to store up a different kind of treasure.

## Session Introduction (10 MINUTES)

Welcome to the first session of *Living Well Spending Less*. If your fellow group members do not know one another, take a few minutes to introduce yourselves. Then, to get things started, discuss one of the following questions:

- What do you hope to learn from this study?
- Are you more intrigued by the idea of "living well" or the idea of "spending less"? Where do you think you need the most help?

## Watch the Video (15 MINUTES)

*Play the* Living Well Spending Less *video segment titled "What Is the Good Life?" As you watch, fill in the blanks in the following outline to help you recall the main concepts presented.*

The good life is not just about learning to spend less, but about actually changing the desires of our _____, shifting our priorities from wanting and hoping for the best of everything in this world to deeply longing to store up a different kind of _____.

How would our perspective change if we took just a few moments to determine what it is we want most out of _____?

True contentment will never be found by looking _____.

Combat discontentment with an attitude of _____.

We need to fervently _____ that God will change our hearts and take away our desire for _____           .

---

**Fill-in answers (in order):** heart, treasure, life, outward, gratitude, pray, the things of this world

---

*Opening Prayer*

> *Lord, each of us is on a journey of transformation. We want to live well, but so often we chase after those things that cannot satisfy us. Help us to long for a different type of richness, a richness that comes only from fullness in Christ. In this study, reveal to each of us the areas where we need you to change our heart so that we can take hold of the life that is truly life. Help us to be honest and accountable to one another in the areas where we need to change, and use this study and this group to help us grow closer to you. Amen.*

## Icebreaker: Image Appeal (10 MINUTES)

For this activity, each participant will need construction paper, scissors, a glue stick, and a stack of women's magazines. Set a timer for three minutes. As quickly as possible, each participant should page through a magazine, tear out the images that appeal to her most, then glue them to the paper. Have fun with this! Don't try to be artsy; just get something down on paper.

At the end of the three minutes, spend some time holding up your collages and explaining a few of your choices. What do you find appealing about the images you chose?

## Group Discussion (25 MINUTES)

1. Write down and share five "earthly" things you currently want most (be honest!).

    •

    •

    •

    •

    •

2. Write down and share five "heavenly" things you want most.

    •

    •

    •

    •

    •

3. Discuss why it seems easier and more desirable to pursue "earthly" things than "heavenly" things.

4. How does our culture define the good life?

5. Share with the group the area of your life where you most feel the "insatiable desire for more."

*Choose a volunteer to read the following passage aloud to the group:*

But the fruit of the Spirit is love, joy, peace, patience, kindness, goodness, faithfulness, gentleness and self-control. Against such things there is no law (Galatians 5:22–23 NIV 1984).

6. How does Paul define the good life?

7. How does the fruit of the Spirit contribute to the good life? Why?

*Look up 1 Timothy 6:11–12, 17–19 and choose a volunteer to read it aloud to the group.*

8. What does God want us to do with what he has given us? What will the result be?

*Closing Prayer*

> *Lord, please take away our desire for the things of this world. Help us to stop longing for everything that distracts our attention from what you want us to experience. Help us to stop trying to fill our lives with things that just don't satisfy. Forgive us for wanting anything other than exactly what you have provided, because that is enough. Amen.*

# Personal Study

*Dig deeper into the material covered in this week's video teaching by engaging in the following between-sessions activities. Be sure to make a few notes in your guide about the experience. There will be a time for you to share these reflections at the beginning of the next group session.*

**Read and Reflect**
Philippians 4:4
1 Timothy 6:9–11

**Book Time**
For more inspiration and practical help, read chapters 1–2 of *Living Well Spending Less*.

## Activity 1: Define the Good Life

Our culture wants us to define the good life in material and experiential ways. But as the fruit of the Spirit has shown us, God has a very different definition of what constitutes the good life. You will find another picture of God's version of the good life in Colossians 3:12–14:

Therefore, as God's chosen people, holy and dearly loved, clothe yourselves with compassion, kindness, humility, gentleness and patience. Bear
with each other and forgive one another if any of you has a grievance
against someone. Forgive as the Lord forgave you. And over all these
virtues put on love, which binds them all together in perfect unity.

➤ List the five behavioral characteristics of God's chosen people (verse 12).

   1.

   2.

   3.

   4.

   5.

Paul tells us to "put on love." Imagine yourself for a few moments getting ready
in the morning *wearing* kindness, *putting on* patience, *buttoning up* humility, *wrap-
ping yourself in* gentleness, *stepping into* compassion. Now that you are *clothed* in
God's virtues, do you feel any *more* or any *less* content in your current circumstances?
(circle *more* or *less*)

➤ How does that image of yourself change your perspective of the good life?

➤ Now let's take another look at the fruit of the Spirit, but this time list the
**opposite** for each of these fruits.

    Love: _____

    Joy: _____

    Peace: _____

    Patience: _____

    Kindness: _____

Goodness: _____

Faithfulness: _____

Gentleness: _____

Self-Control: _____

Looking at this list, what fruit of the Spirit do you most struggle to exhibit? Write that word on a notecard and place it where you'll see it often (desk, dashboard, or kitchen sink). For at least three days, pray that God will grow that fruit in your life, and take note of the result.

*Day #1:*

*Day #2:*

*Day #3:*

➤ **List the things you desire that interfere with your ability to live the good life as God defines it.**

Your perspective and desires affect the very things God says matter most—your ability to experience and exhibit peace, joy, love, and kindness. If you want to transform your perspective and desires, you will need the help of the Holy Spirit, and to access that help you will need to pray often. Prayer is the one secret weapon you have as you begin your journey to *Living Well* and *Spending Less* because prayer is what keeps our hearts and minds tethered to what matters to God.

In Mark 11:24, Jesus told his disciples, "Therefore I tell you, whatever you ask for in prayer, believe that you have received it, and it will be yours."

Take a minute and pray that God will help you change and refine your definition of the good life to be more in line with his.

## Activity 2: Stop Looking!

Our culture keeps us restlessly looking, hooked into an endless "desire loop," stoking our desires and promising fulfillment if we indulge them. Spend a day or two noting the times when your desires are enflamed and you find yourself feeling envious and wanting more. Is there a person, group, activity, or situation that triggers this emotion? For example: reading blogs, paging through women's magazines, watching HGTV, browsing Facebook or Pinterest, shopping at the mall, working out at the gym, attending kids' sports events, meeting up with certain friends, and so on.

> ➤ **Write those situations here:**

If you can, limit your time or block your exposure to that activity or person for the next three days or until your group meets again. Then note your emotions. Return to page 21 every day and note the difference you are experiencing: Do you see a change? Are you able to quiet the discontent in your heart?

➤ What I stopped or blocked exposure to:

➤ How it made me feel:

➤ What I stopped or blocked exposure to:

➤ How it made me feel:

➤ What I stopped or blocked exposure to:

➤ How it made me feel:

➤ Read Proverbs 17:24. What does this tell you about the importance of "training your gaze"? Where should your focus be?

➤ Read Ephesians 1:18. Why do you think we need to pray for enlightenment in order to keep our focus on God's riches instead of the world's riches?

➤ Read 1 John 2:16. What is the difference between God's riches and the world's riches?

Pray: *Lord, give me wisdom. Please help me spot those situations that cause me to take my eyes off you. Replace the lust of my eyes and flesh with a passion for your presence. Remind me of the priceless inheritance you have already given me and make me grateful. Amen.*

## Activity 3: Conclusion and Reflection

We've spent this week thinking about the good life and how it is defined, both by this world and by God. In light of what you've learned, reflect on the following questions:

➤ Before this week or before you met Jesus, how did you define the good life?

➤ In what ways has your definition of the good life changed, either since studying this lesson or since meeting Jesus?

➤ Name the fruit of the Spirit you pursued this week. What, if anything, did you give up in order to receive that fruit?

➤ Read again 1 Timothy 6:17–19. What do these verses mean to you?

➤ To battle discontent, consciously cultivate an attitude of gratitude. List three things for which you are thankful.

Use the space below to write any key points, realizations, or questions you want to bring to the next group meeting.

# Finding Your Sweet Spot

The sweet spot is the place where our passion and ability intersect, enabling us to do great things for the kingdom of God.

## Opening Reflection (5 MINUTES)

Spend some time sharing your thoughts and reflections from last week's session or personal study. Is there an experience or realization that stood out to you? Did you make progress in some area?

## Session Introduction (5 MINUTES)

To get things started, discuss one of the following questions:

- Think of one super-successful, ultra-driven, goal-oriented person in your life. You know the type. She's talented and courageous and smart and beautiful. She's got everything going for her, while you seemingly have nothing. But have you ever stopped to think about what sets her and other go-getters apart from the rest of us? The happiest, most successful, and most fulfilled people *do* have a secret road map for their lives. What might be included on that map?
- Think about your passion—the activity that makes you jump out of bed in the morning, or rush home from work just so you can have a little more time for it. If you could do only one thing right now, what would it be?

## Watch the Video (17 MINUTES)

*Play the* Living Well Spending Less *video segment titled "Finding Your Sweet Spot." As you watch, fill in the blanks in the following outline to help you recall the main concepts presented.*

Living in our _____ means taking the time to discover our _____ and being willing to take the next _____.

Written goals can change your life.

Here are a few practical tips for effective and concrete goal setting:

    i.  Be clear about your _____.

   ii.  Give yourself a _____.

  iii.  Break down large _____.

  iv.  Track your _____.

   v.  Create _____.

  vi.  Celebrate _____.

If we are serious about attaining our goals we must make the daily choice to do something.

Creating good _____ is the key to being able to get things done.

---

**Fill-in answers (in order):** sweet spot, passions, step, objective, due date, goals, progress, accountability, success, habits

---

*Opening Prayer*

> *Lord Jesus, we all long to know not only who we are but also how we can make our lives count. We know that you have given each of us gifts and talents, but too often we either fail to recognize them or we fail to nurture and train them into full fruitfulness. Forgive us for all the good things we have left undone. Give us the insight to know who we are, the courage and self-discipline to shape who we are for the good you have prepared us to do, and the joy of finding our strength in you along the way. Amen.*

## Icebreaker: Goal Setting Mad Libs (10 MINUTES)

Have you ever enjoyed a game of Mad Libs with a group of friends? In this fun word game, a leader prompts the group for a list of words to substitute for blanks in a story, then reads the often comical or nonsensical story aloud, using the supplied words. Let's use Mad Libs to start our discussion on how to set and achieve goals. Write down an answer to the following three questions. Be silly or serious—your choice!

1. I would like to . . . (*name a goal* _____)
2. I plan to do it by . . . (*name a step toward that goal* _____)
3. To celebrate the achievement of my goal I'm going to . . . (*name a reward* _____)

Now the leader will read each sentence stem aloud, then point to a *different* group member each time for the answer. The results might sound like this:

*I would like to* . . . (Member #1) "lose ten pounds."
*I plan to do it by* . . . (Member #2) "calling a contractor."
*To celebrate the achievement of my goal I'm going to* . . . (Member #3) "shoot off fireworks!"

In other words, the results should sound a bit crazy! Repeat the process several more times for the fun of it.

Too often, goal setting can seem serious and intimidating. Discuss briefly how we can instead approach goal setting with anticipation, joy, and yes, even some laughter. How might cultivating a positive attitude help us achieve our goals?

## Group Discussion (25 MINUTES)

1. Finding your sweet spot often involves a messy process of discovering and then learning to embrace the God-given talents and aptitudes you *already have* rather than the ones you *wish* you had. What talent do you have that seems unimportant? Why?

2. What talent do you wish you had instead? Why?

*Select a volunteer to read the following passage aloud to the group:*

> There are different kinds of gifts, but the same Spirit distributes them. There are different kinds of service, but the same Lord. There are different kinds of working, but in all of them and in everyone it is the same God at work (1 Corinthians 12:4–6).

3. Go around the group and have each person name a service she believes she offers to others and how she has seen God at work through that service.

4. Now go around the group and have each person name one way that another person's service in the past week was a blessing to her. For example, someone may be grateful for a teen's help with a computer problem, or someone might be thankful for a friend's word of encouragement during a tough time.

5. Discuss how you felt when you heard each group member describe her service or the way she was served. How does it help you to know that God is at work through many different kinds of gifts, service, and work?

6. How can we help each other recognize and use our gifts in service to God and one another?

*Closing Prayer*

> *Lord, help us to find our sweet spot, the place where our passion and ability intersect in such a way that we can make an impact on the world for good, to please and serve you. Help us to set goals that will keep us focused and productive, not just to advance our own agenda but to bring forth your kingdom on earth. We love you, Lord! Amen.*

# Personal Study

Dig deeper into the material covered in this week's video teaching by engaging in the following between-sessions activities. Be sure to make a few notes in your guide about the experience. There will be a time for you to share these reflections at the beginning of the next group session.

---

**Read and Reflect**
1 Corinthians 12:4–6
Philippians 4:13

**Book Time**
For more inspiration and practical help, read chapters 3–4 of *Living Well Spending Less*.

---

### Activity 1: Exploring Your Passions

Passions can be a good thing, giving us the impetus to pursue our goals and accomplish great things. But they can be a bad thing if they are misplaced or misguided.

The Bible talks about passions as "zeal" or "fervor." Romans 12:11 says, "Never be lacking in zeal, but keep your spiritual fervor, serving the Lord." And Galatians 4:18 says, "It is fine to be zealous, provided the purpose is good."

➤ What do these verses teach you about the place of zeal (passion) in your life?

➤ When do you experience spiritual fervor? What might that tell you about where you can best serve the Lord?

➤ Describe a time when your zeal was misplaced or misguided. What was the result?

➤ If you are "lacking in zeal," pray now that God will rekindle your passion to love and serve him. If you have a current passion, write it here and prayerfully examine whether its purpose is good.

➤ In 2 Corinthian 5:9, Paul says, "We make it our goal to please [Christ]." Why should pleasing Christ be your primary goal?

➤ How does this ultimate goal—of pleasing Christ—help to shape your day-to-day passions and goals?

➤ Paul goes on to say, "For we must all appear before the judgment seat of Christ, so that each of us may receive what is due us for the things done while in the body, whether good or bad" (2 Corinthians 5:10). Does it make you feel uncomfortable to think of a time of judgment? How does this knowledge of a coming judgment day change your perspective on success, time management, and goal setting?

## Activity 2: Set a Goal

It's not enough to have a vision in your head of what you wish you could accomplish. You need to *write it down*. Taking the time to write down your goals will motivate you to act on them. Use this activity to practice the five steps for setting and achieving a goal. For the purposes of this activity, we will confine the process to one week (or however long it is till your next group session), but once you have gone through these five steps and achieved your goal, consider using this process for another, perhaps larger goal.

### Step One: Define a Goal

What goal would you like to achieve before the next group session? Write your goal here. Make sure it is concrete and quantifiable so that you can be crystal clear that you have achieved it. For example, saying "I want to plan our family vacation" is not as clear or quantifiable as saying "I want to research options and book a destination for our spring break trip."

### Step Two: Give Yourself a Due Date

To motivate yourself and combat a tendency to procrastinate, write down a due date for achieving your goal (choose a date that is *before* your next group session).

_____

### Step Three: Define Your Steps

Write down the specific steps you need to take to get to your goal. Give yourself deadlines for each of those steps.

### Step Four: Create Accountability

Tell someone about the goal you want to achieve and how you hope to achieve it. Who will you tell?

_____

### Step Five: Celebrate Success

Come to the next group session prepared to share what your goal was and how you achieved it!

Now let's take this five-step goal setting process and apply it to our spiritual life. Read Philippians 3:12–14 for Paul's take on goal setting.

### Step One: Define a Goal

According to Paul, what is our big life goal?

### Step Two: Give Yourself a Due Date

According to Paul, what is the deadline for that goal?

### Step Three: Define Your Steps

What specific steps can you take *this week* that will help get you to that goal? Hint: Think of some things you will need to "forget," and name ways that you can "press on."

### Step Four: Create Accountability

Who was holding Paul accountable for achieving his goal? (Hint: he was writing to them!)

Who holds you spiritually accountable? Write their name(s) here:

_____

_____

_____

### Step Five: Celebrate Success

Paul celebrates spiritual success by writing about it in his letters to the churches (for one example, see Ephesians 1:15–16). What can you do *right now* to celebrate the progress you've already made in your journey with Jesus? For example: journal about it, light a candle and meditate, or sing a praise and worship song. Now do it!

## Activity 3: Conclusion and Reflection

Understanding our gifts and passions and setting and achieving goals are all well and good, but even the most optimized and successful life will be ultimately worthless if we forget to include God. In light of what you've learned so far, reflect on the following questions:

➤ Think about your dreams and passions. What do you love to do most of all?

➤ Read Luke 12:13–21. What was this man's gift?

➤ What was his passion?

➤ What goal did he set?

➤ How did he plan to celebrate the achievement of his goal?

➤ What did God think of this man and his plans?

➤ Read Psalm 37:4. Be honest, who or what is the source of your desires? And how might that source end up affecting what you desire?

➤ Read Exodus 30:30–35 where Moses describes Bezalel. List five gifts that God gave Bezalel which are general enough to apply to anyone (including you!). Pray and ask God, who gives generously to those who ask, for those same gifts.

➤ Like Bezalel, God has also blessed you with some specific skills. List those skills here. How does God use those skills now, and how might he use them in the future in new ways?

➤ Next listen to the whispers of holy discontentment in your life. Is there something you've always wanted to do but haven't gathered the nerve to try? Do you have the feeling you are on the wrong path? What would it take to make a change?

➤ Read John 16:13. As you face an uncertain future—wondering where to use your gifts, talents, and passions, and what goals you should set—what does this verse tell you about where you can find help, and what kind of help it will be? Pray and ask for that help now.

Use the space below to write any key points, realizations, or questions you want to bring to the next group meeting.

# Develop Good Habits

We demonstrate godly wisdom when
we develop good habits for budgeting,
grocery shopping, and cleaning.

## Opening Reflection (5 MINUTES)

Spend some time sharing your thoughts and reflections from last week's session or personal study. Is there an experience or realization that stood out to you? Did you make progress in some area?

## Session Introduction (5 MINUTES)

In our last session we talked about the importance of setting goals. In this session we are going to delve into three important habits—living on a budget, saving on groceries, and keeping a clean and tidy home. Keeping our homes running smoothly is a practical way to demonstrate godly wisdom, as Proverbs 31 shows us. However, we all have areas where we are weak and prone to failure. Briefly answer one of the following questions:

- In the arenas of budgeting, grocery shopping, and keeping house, what is your weakness?
- What do you love to buy that you shouldn't buy?
- What cleaning chore do you hate to do that you should be doing more often?

## Watch the Video (13 MINUTES)

*Play the* Living Well Spending Less *video segment titled "Develop Good Habits." As you watch, fill in the blanks in the following outline to help you recall the main concepts presented.*

Peace is defined in the dictionary as "a state in which there is no _____ or fighting; a state of tranquility or freedom from disquieting or oppressive thoughts or emotions; harmony in personal relations; _____."

Financial peace is a state of _____.

Financial peace starts with _____ and a change in our _____.

Budgeting involves identifying your _____ and your fixed and variable _____.

Extreme grocery savings do not come from coupons but from buying food when it is at its lowest possible _____.

A clean house makes it nice to simply be at _____. Our home can be a haven, an oasis from the hustle and bustle of life.

---

**Fill-in answers (in order):** war, contentment, mind, prayer, heart, income, expenses, price, home

---

*Opening Prayer*

> *Lord Jesus, you know how we struggle with the daily details of our lives. We want to make and keep a budget; we want to eat healthy, home-cooked meals; and we'd love to have a clean and tidy home—but so many things get in our way! You have given us all these resources to enjoy—our money, our food, our home. Now help us to steward them well and honor you in all we do. Amen.*

## Icebreaker: Best Practices (10 MINUTES)

When it comes to managing our homes, few of us are good at *everything*, but all of us are good at *something*. Write down an answer to at least one of the following questions. Then share your answers. Take note of each other's tips and skills; you may learn something!

- When it comes to budgeting, my best practice is . . . _____
- The way I save on groceries is . . . ._____
- I keep a clean and tidy house by . . . _____

The daily chores of budgeting, shopping, cooking, and cleaning are not rewarded with paychecks or much if any recognition. In what ways does your faith help you persevere when "the daily grind" gets you down?

## Group Discussion (25 MINUTES)

1. Financial peace can be defined as "a state of mutual harmony with money; freedom from oppressive thoughts or emotions related to spending; harmony in personal relationships and freedom from strife or dissension regarding personal finances; contentment with what one has." What oppressive thoughts or emotions have you had related to spending or budgeting? Why?

2. How does money or budgeting affect your personal relationships?

*Read the following passage:*

> But godliness with contentment is great gain. For we brought nothing into the world, and we can take nothing out of it (1 Timothy 6:6–7).

3. How does godliness help us to stay content?

4. Why are godliness and contentment so important, such that Paul calls them a "great gain"?

*Read the following passage:*

> Come, all you who are thirsty,
>> come to the waters;
> and you who have no money,
>> come, buy and eat!
> Come, buy wine and milk
>> without money and without cost.
> Why spend money on what is not bread,
>> and your labor on what does not satisfy?
> Listen, listen to me, and eat what is good,
>> and you will delight in the richest of fare.
> Give ear and come to me;
>> listen, that you may live" (Isaiah 55:1–3).

5. How does this passage help you to put your grocery shopping in perspective?

6. Jesus declared, "I am the bread of life. Whoever comes to me will never go hungry, and whoever believes in me will never be thirsty" (John 6:35). How has knowing Jesus helped you to satisfy some hunger inside of you?

7. If you have a smart phone, go to BibleGateway.com, type in the word *clean*, and quickly scan the resulting verses. The Old Testament includes numerous rules that God's people had to follow to be considered ceremonially clean; that is, to be able to approach God. Why do you think God taught his people to value cleanliness? How does keeping a clean body and a clean house help us?

### Closing Prayer

*Lord, we are so grateful for what you've given us. Help us to find peace not in the numbers in our bank account but in you. Help us to fill our hunger, not with food or trinkets, but with your Spirit. Now, as we face the ceaseless, daily demands of budgeting, shopping, cooking, and cleaning, keep us focused and motivated, joyful and self-disciplined, thankful and resourceful, hard-working and faithful. In Jesus' name we pray. Amen.*

# Personal Study

Dig deeper into the material covered in this week's video teaching by engaging in the following between-sessions activities. Be sure to make a few notes in your guide about the experience. There will be a time for you to share these reflections at the beginning of the next group session.

---

**Read and Reflect**
Proverbs 31:10–31

**Book Time**
For more inspiration and practical help, read chapters 8–10 of *Living Well Spending Less*.

---

## Activity 1: The Values of Money

The way we spend our money will reflect our deepest values. On the next page, track your spending by writing down every purchase you make for five days (use additional paper if needed). Then after you've tracked your spending, come back and answer the following questions.

*Day #1*

*Day #2*

*Day #3*

*Day #4*

*Day #5*

➤ **What does your spending reveal about what you value?**

➤ Are your values in alignment with God's priorities? See Matthew 6:33.
How would you define the kingdom of God? How does that differ from the
kingdom of the world?

God instituted the tithe as a way for us to show that we value him above all
other things. By giving a tenth of what we earn to the church and kingdom causes,
we demonstrate our obedience to God, our trust that he will provide, and our
gratitude for all he has given us. See Malachi 3:8–10.

➤ What happens when we don't tithe?

➤ What does God promise when we do tithe faithfully?

First Timothy 5:8 teaches us another important value in terms of how we spend
our money.

➤ What is this value, and how did your spending this week reflect this value?
Remember, this value is equally applicable to the single and married!

➤ In what ways did your spending this past week fall short of this value?

➤ Is there an area of spending that will cause you to become poor if you keep it up? See Proverbs 21:17.

➤ What will help you to maintain self-control? See Titus 2:11–14.

As you reflect on your spending over this past week, pray the following prayer: *Lord, I want to put you first and to be responsible in my spending, but so often I put my own desires and pleasures first, without thought for you or the needs of others. Forgive me for my selfishness. Change my heart so that I will value what you value. Open my eyes to ways I can change my spending to better reflect my love for you and those you have asked me to care for. Amen.*

## Activity 2: Proverbs and Money

The book of Proverbs has a lot to say about how we handle money. Reflect on the following passages, noting areas where you feel convicted or encouraged in your handling of money. How do these proverbs confront or challenge the prevailing wisdom on riches?

➤ According to Proverbs 8:18, how do we become prosperous?

➤ Read Proverbs 1:7. How do we become wise? Why do we need to start here?

➤ According to Proverbs 11:28, what happens to those who trust in their riches? How can you tell if you trust God more than your job, your pension, your retirement fund, your investment adviser, or your ability to manage your budget?

➤ According to Proverbs 23:4, what are some dangers we face as we work to make money?

➤ According to Proverbs 28:20, what goal will be punished? What goal will be blessed? If you are faithful, what blessings are you currently enjoying? If you aren't, how might God be disciplining you to show you a better way to live?

➤ Proverbs 13:7 reminds us how deceptive appearances can be. Write down the two kinds of people mentioned in the verse. Which kind of person do you pretend to be? Why?

➤ Proverbs 28:22 reminds us that big spenders are not the only people who live in danger of poverty. Who else should be worried, according to this verse? Did the answer surprise you? Why?

➤ Our culture runs on debt, from student loans to car payments to credit cards to mortgages. What does Proverbs 22:7 say about debt? Do you view debt in this drastic and dramatic way? Why or why not? How would it help you to take this view of debt?

➤ Proverbs 23:5 gives a powerful and even humorous view of riches. How does this picture help you put money into perspective?

Now look at your answers to the previous questions with an eye to filling in the blanks to the following prayer. Then pray it like you mean it! *Lord, as I read your wisdom on money, I spotted places where my heart and behavior were out of alignment with your loving words of truth. I have trouble with _____ and with _____. Now that I am aware of those issues in my life, please give me the tools I need to address them: godly knowledge, self-control, and accountability. Thank you for caring about the details of my life, even the way I make and spend each dollar. You only want the best for me—and the best is your Son, Jesus. Amen.*

## Activity 3: Conclusion and Reflection

As we think about the areas of budgeting, shopping, and keeping house, we need to keep in mind a few other principles.

➤ Read Philippians 2:14–15. It says you should do everything—and that would include budgeting, shopping, and keeping house—without what? Why is that?

➤ If you examine the ways you manage your money and your household, in what ways is your behavior or attitude just as "warped and crooked" as the current culture? What do you wish was different? Write it here. Then write a brief plan of attack. How can you work to change that behavior or attitude **this week**?

➤ In what ways does your behavior depart from the way the world behaves? Is there an area where you shine? Think of a way you can use that trait or behavior to help someone else this week, and then write it here.

We learned in session one how important an attitude of gratitude is toward living a good life. In session two we learned the importance of goals. So now let's look at how an attitude of gratitude and a goal (mission) can transform your approach to budgeting, grocery shopping, and house cleaning.

### Budgeting

Write a prayer here that mentions one of your current budgeting challenges—do so in the context of gratitude and mission. Be specific! For example: *Lord, I'm thankful for this new electronic budgeting program that helps me track my spending, but I'm not using it as faithfully as I should. Help me to work on it each morning so I can find more money to give to my church.*

### Grocery Shopping

Write a prayer here that mentions your grocery shopping. Be grateful, specific, and mission minded. For example: *Lord, I love to buy fresh produce at the farmers' market! Thank you for all the farmers there who remind me of the hard work that goes into growing and harvesting healthy food. As I meet and greet each farmer today, help me to show them how much you love them.*

### House Cleaning

Write a prayer here that mentions a cleaning chore. Be grateful, specific, and mission minded. For example: *Lord, I don't always love doing laundry, but I adore the people who make it! Thank you for the gift of my family. Help me to find joy in serving them, as you called me to serve.*

Use the space below to write any key points, realizations, or questions you want to bring to the next group meeting.

# Less Stuff Equals More Joy

Love of things can easily consume us,
but in truth, the best things in life are free.

## Opening Reflection (5 MINUTES)

Spend some time sharing your thoughts and reflections from last week's session or personal study. Is there an experience or realization that stood out to you? Did you make progress in some area?

## Session Introduction (5 MINUTES)

In our last three sessions we examined God's definition of the good life, learned how to set goals (especially the ultimate goal), and explored how our handling of money reveals our values. By now you should be able to identify areas in your heart and life where change might be needed. Today we will look at how "living well" might mean "spending less" on stuff—and how having less can actually equal more joy.

We have been so blessed by prosperity that sometimes our homes are stuffed! Spend a few minutes talking about your relationship with "stuff." Briefly answer one of these questions:

- What do you tend to collect, covet, want more of all the time? Where have you been frustrated in your attempts to pare back?
- Why do you think the Bible makes it so clear that "treasure" can be stored here on earth or in heaven?

## Watch the Video (17 MINUTES)

*Play the* Living Well Spending Less *video segment titled "Less Stuff Equals More Joy." As you watch, fill in the blanks in the following outline to help you recall the main concepts presented.*

Paring down our stuff can often create more contentment and appreciation and enjoyment of what we have.

_____ isn't bad or dangerous in and of itself, but in a world where we are constantly told that what we have isn't quite _____ enough, the _____ of things can so easily consume us.

The parable of the bags of gold teaches us that with many _____ comes much responsibility.

When it comes right down to it, the _____ things in life really are absolutely _____.

Romans 12:13 says, "Share with the Lord's people who are in _____. Practice hospitality."

If living well means having _____ but appreciating _____, focusing on the best things in life that are free, then I can't help thinking this is the best _____ of all.

---

**Fill-in answers (in order):** stuff, good, love, blessings, best, free, need, less, more, gift

---

*Opening Prayer*

*Lord Jesus, you have blessed us with an abundance of all we could ever need. In fact, sometimes that abundance overwhelms and engulfs us! Help us to be faithful stewards of our stuff, giving away what we no longer need, sharing what we have, and choosing carefully what we bring into our homes. Instead of focusing on acquiring more stuff, help us to treasure hospitality and friendship and kindness. In Jesus' name we pray. Amen.*

## Icebreaker: Overstuffed (10 MINUTES)

We all struggle to tame at least one area of our home, whether that be our junk drawer, kids' playroom, storage area, kitchen pantry, or walk-in closet. Take a moment to share what area of your home is currently your biggest challenge in terms of keeping it uncluttered and organized. Why is this area so prone to chaos? How might this chaos affect your relationship with God and others?

## Group Discussion (25 MINUTES)

1. At one point, Ruth made a decision to take away all her daughters' toys. What did you think of her decision? Could you do that to your children? What do you think would happen if you did?

*Read the following passage:*

> Do not store up for yourselves treasures on earth, where moth and rust destroy and where thieves break in and steal, but store up for yourselves treasures in heaven, where moth and rust do not destroy and where thieves do not break in and steal. For where your treasure is, there will your heart be also (Matthew 6:19–21 NIV 1984).

2. Think of an "earthly treasure" that was lost, stolen, or damaged somehow. How did that experience affect your attitude toward your possessions?

3. Our culture is finding that possessions can be as much of a bane as a blessing. As a result, instead of collecting stuff, many people have begun to collect experiences. Go around the room and have each participant name what "bucket list" experience they would like to have before they die.

4. Should "bucket list" experiences also be considered "treasures on earth"? If so, how can we be mindful in our pursuit of them?

5. Be honest with yourself. Where is your treasure? Where is your heart? Take a moment to pray silently, repenting for any idol you may have treasured more than Jesus himself.

6. Romans 12:13 says, "Share with the Lord's people who are in need. Practice hospitality." Sometimes the need may be financial, but sometimes it may be emotional. Share a story of a time you showed hospitality to someone who was poor, lonely, sick, grieving, or struggling. Why did you feel compelled to help?

*Closing Prayer*

> *Lord, sometimes we are so overwhelmed with all the "stuff" we have to manage that we forget to pursue the things that really matter. Instead of storing up treasures here on earth—all the stuff that can break and all the memories that will fade—help us to store up treasures in heaven. Help us to cherish all the good things you've given that are free: love, friendship, kindness, and hospitality, to name just a few. May we seek to purchase fewer things and experiences and instead appreciate more of what you have already given us, especially the great gift of your Son, Jesus. Amen.*

# Personal Study

Dig deeper into the material covered in this week's video teaching by engaging in the following between-sessions activities. Be sure to make a few notes in your guide about the experience. There will be a time for you to share these reflections at the beginning of the next group session.

---

**Read and Reflect**
Matthew 25:35–40

**Book Time**
For more inspiration and practical help, read chapters 6–7 and 11 of *Living Well Spending Less*.

---

## Activity 1: Deadly Greed

Two stories in the Bible dramatically illustrate the deadly consequences of greed. One is found in the Old Testament, and one is found in the New.

➤ Read the story of Achan in Joshua 7. What sin was God trying to root out? See verse 11.

➤ Now read Joshua 6, especially verses 17–19. Jericho was the first city that Israel conquered when it entered the Promised Land. As such, it was a "first fruit" (tithe) to be dedicated to God. What does this tell you about the seriousness of Achan's act?

➤ Read the story of Ananias and Sapphira in Acts 5:1–11. What was their sin?

➤ The story of Ananias and Sapphira occurs at the very beginning of the church, just as the story of Achan occurs at the very beginning of the nation of Israel. Why were these stories recorded for us? For hints, see Acts 5:5, 11.

➤ Have you ever heard the phrase "scared straight"? How does fear motivate us?

While our greed may not literally kill us, it can have serious consequences. Consider these commonly experienced consequences of greed:

- Bankruptcy
- Divorce
- Broken relationships
- Loneliness
- Anxiety and depression
- Addiction and ill health
- Imprisonment

➤ **Think of someone you know who was destroyed by some form of greed. What steps did they take down the wrong path? What can you learn from their story?**

Consider your possessions. Is there something that stands out as an example of your greediness? Consider selling it or giving it away in order to tune your heart into God's values.

Or, as an exercise in battling greed, choose an area of your house that you would like to declutter and organize. Follow these steps, and for accountability, report the results to your group next week by taking a "before" and "after photo" of that area.

1. Do an initial sweep. Take a box or large garbage bag and quickly grab anything that either is garbage or no longer needed.
2. Second, focus on what's left and ruthlessly purge. Give yourself permission to keep only the things that are currently useful. As you sort through your things, ask yourself these questions:
   - Do we use it, wear it, or play with it?
   - If it is clothing, does it still fit?
   - Is it in good working condition?
   - Does it enrich our lives in some way?

- Does it have sentimental value?
- Could someone else use it more?
- Am I treasuring this item more than heavenly treasure?

3. Third, get the discarded stuff out of your house. Once you've determined that something needs to go, get rid of it as quickly as possible. Don't let the boxes of donation items or the pile of things you plan to sell sit around your garage or basement for months on end.

➤ **Reflect on your experience. How did your awareness of the dangers of greed help you in your quest to declutter?**

In your battle against greed, pray the words of Proverbs 30:8: *Lord, keep falsehood and lies far from me; give me neither poverty nor riches, but give me only my daily bread.*

## Activity 2: More Jesus = Less Stuff

Jesus himself had something to say about our pursuit of the good life and earthly possessions. Reflect on his words, noting areas where they touch a particular challenge you are facing. How do his words confront the prevailing wisdom on how we handle our daily needs? Write down your thoughts on the next page.

Therefore I tell you, do not worry about your life, what you will eat or drink; or about your body, what you will wear. Is not life more than food, and the body more than clothes? (Matthew 6:25).

➤ Think about your food worries and write one here.

➤ Imagine Jesus talking to you about that worry. Write what he says here.

➤ Think about your clothing worries and write one here.

➤ Imagine Jesus talking to you about that worry. Write what he says here.

➤ How do Jesus' words "Is not life more than food, and the body more than clothes" help you to put things in perspective?

So do not worry, saying, "What shall we eat?" or "What shall we drink?" or "What shall we wear?" For the pagans run after all these things, and your heavenly Father knows that you need them (Matthew 6:31–32).

➤ In what ways have you acted like a pagan and "run after all these things"? Be specific.

➤ How did this "running" make you feel?

➤ How does it help you to realize that "your heavenly Father knows that you need" food, clothing, and other necessities of life?

But seek first his kingdom and his righteousness, and all these things will be given to you as well (Matthew 6:33).

➤ How do God's priorities differ from the world's priorities?

➤ Why does God want us to put his kingdom and his righteousness first in our lives?

➤ What does he promise he will give us if we put him first? What are "these things"? (Hint: see Matthew 6:25, 31–32, above.)

Watch out! Be on your guard against all kinds of greed; life does not consist in an abundance of possessions (Luke 12:15).

➤ Why did Jesus warn us so sharply against greed? (Hint: see Activity #1!)

➤ Name some kinds of greed you have observed. Then name the types of greed you struggle with most.

➤ How can you be on guard against the particular kind of greed that plagues you? Be specific!

Now take a minute to slowly and thoughtfully pray the Lord's Prayer, paying special attention to the phrases "your kingdom come," "give us this day our daily bread," and "lead us not into temptation." Let these phrases help you recalibrate your heart to God's values and God's truth.

## Activity 3: Conclusion and Reflection

Jesus knew that our relationship with stuff would inevitably affect our relationships with God and other people. For example, if we work overtime in order to have more stuff or to pursue our "bucket list," we have less time to pray, attend church activities, or care for our friends and family. If we seek to impress people with our stuff and experiences, we will alienate them. If we horde our stuff and spend our money wastefully, we harm those who need these things more than we do. That's why practicing hospitality is such a great way to battle greed and the compulsion to have and do more.

Read the story of Mary and Martha in Luke 10:38–42.

➤ **What was Martha concerned about?**

➤ **What was Mary concerned about?**

➤ **What does this tell you about who or what we should prioritize when we practice hospitality?**

Romans 12:13 says, "Share with the Lord's people who are in need. Practice hospitality." Choose one of the following activities to practice friendship and heartfelt hospitality this week.

• Make plans to visit with a friend you haven't seen in a while. If they are out of town, contact them and make a phone date.
• Make a list of your friends, and then spend time praying for them.

- Host a dinner or some other social gathering; instead of seeking Pinterest perfection, smile, listen, and focus on making your guests feel warmly welcomed.
- Reach out to someone who is sick, housebound, new to your town or church, or struggling in some way.
- Purchase or bake a treat to share with someone: your colleagues, neighbors, classmates, or next week's session attendees!

Use the space below to write any key points, realizations, or questions you want to bring to the next group meeting.

In our study of *Living Well Spending Less*, we've looked at the good life and how to define and attain it; we've talked about the importance of setting goals and keeping our focus on kingdom values; and we've discussed how to break the hold that money and possessions have upon us. In the next four sessions based on Ruth's book *Unstuffed*, we will take a closer look at how we can better manage our hearts and our households to demonstrate kingdom priorities and godly wisdom. See you next week!

# Home

Create a vision for your house and
heart that will help you declutter.

## Opening Reflection (5 MINUTES)

Spend some time sharing your thoughts and reflections from last week's session or personal study. Is there an experience or realization that stood out to you? Did you make progress in some area?

## Session Introduction (5 MINUTES)

In our study of *Living Well Spending Less*, we looked at the good life and how to define it and attain it; we talked about the importance of setting goals and keeping our focus on kingdom values; and we discussed how to break the hold that money and possessions have upon us. In these next four sessions based on Ruth's book *Unstuffed*, we will take a closer look at how we can better manage our hearts and our households to demonstrate kingdom priorities and godly wisdom. Let's start by taking a look at our homes.

In our last session we began to look at our "junk," literally—all the stuff that clutters our closets and cupboards. In the four sessions of *Unstuffed*, we'll take our decluttering to the next level, looking at how we can pare back our overly cluttered hearts, homes, and schedules, and instead focus on what really matters. Let's start by taking a look at our homes.

Briefly answer the following question:

- Have you ever walked into someone else's house and immediately felt at home? Like somehow, even though it wasn't really yours, you just belonged there? Describe briefly what you saw and consider what made you feel that way.

## Watch the Video (14 MINUTES)

*Play the* Unstuffed *video segment titled "Home." As you watch, fill in the blanks in the following outline to help you recall the main concepts presented.*

We need to start eliminating _____.

We must learn to always stick to the _____.

Fighting every day to prevent new _____ from coming in is the only way to really win the battle against _____.

Keep only that which is currently _____, despite who gave it to us and despite how much it cost.

Get **FREE** of clutter by:

F_____ the flow.

R_____ purging.

E_____ limits.

E_____ quality over quantity.

Proverbs 4:23 says, "Above all else, guard your _____, for everything you do flows from it."

We need to teach our children that money comes from _____.

There's one fundamental truth that our consumer-driven society so desperately wants us to forget: we already have _____.

---

**Fill-in answers (in order):** temptation, essentials, stuff, clutter, useful, fighting, ruthlessly, establishing, emphasizing, heart, work, enough

---

### Opening Prayer

*Lord Jesus, we long for our homes to be havens of peace for ourselves and our loved ones. We long to have our spending under control, to have our values and priorities in the right place, and to teach and model those*

*values to our children. Give us a vision for our home, one that will motivate us to do the hard work needed to create and maintain a happy home. And give us the strength and self-discipline to persevere. Thank you for our homes and families, Jesus, and bless them. Amen.*

## Icebreaker: Clear Out the Clutter! (10 MINUTES)

Last week we challenged you to attack an area of clutter in your home as a way to battle greed (see Activity #1, "Deadly Greed," on pages 59–62). If you have "before" and "after" photos of that experience, share them now, or talk about what you did and how it made you feel. And if you didn't have time last week to declutter, describe another time when you were forced to downsize and discard stuff, perhaps due to a move. How did you feel about your possessions when you had to pack them all up and then unpack them?

## Group Discussion (25 MINUTES)

*Read the following passage:*

> Above all else, guard your heart, for everything you do flows from it (Proverbs 4:23).

1. Ruth notes that "our homes are quite possibly the most open and honest reflection of our state of mind we will ever find." Do you find this to be true? Discuss what your home says about your current state of mind.

2. How might diving down into the "heart" level—discerning your heart's deepest loves and priorities—help you address your state of mind and therefore the state of your home?

*Ask a volunteer to read the following passage aloud to the group:*

> Therefore, since we are surrounded by such a great cloud of witnesses, let us throw off everything that hinders and the sin that so easily entangles. And let us run with perseverance the race marked out for us, fixing our eyes on Jesus, the pioneer and perfecter of faith (Hebrews 12:1–2).

3. Becoming unstuffed ultimately means removing everything that doesn't contribute to the way you want your home to feel, while keeping everything that does. What things would you like to remove from your home? Why? How would removing those things help you to focus more on kingdom values and activities?

4. What may be hindering you in your efforts to manage your home? What sin may be entangling you? Look at the suggestions below and circle one or two:
   - Laziness: Unstuffing is just too much work.
   - Envy: I buy a lot of stuff in order to keep up with my peers.
   - Gluttony: I enjoy having a lot of stuff.
   - Pride: I like to show off my stuff.
   - Despair: I just don't think I can get rid of my stuff.
   - Greed: I want to collect more and more nice stuff.
   - Anger: I am fed up with my family for generating so much stuff.
   - Worry: I'm afraid I may run out of stuff.

For accountability and further insight, take a few minutes to share where you struggle and reflect on why that sin may be dogging you.

5. The Hebrews passage describes Jesus as the "pioneer and perfecter" of our faith. That means Jesus not only blazes the trail for us, showing us the way to go, but he also helps us to become perfect. How does that knowledge help you in your quest to manage your home?

6. Not only do we need to throw out those things we no longer want or need, but we need to actively strive for an end goal. In order to get there, we need a clear picture of what that goal looks like. Take a moment to write down a goal for your home, and then share it with the group. How does keeping your eyes fixed on Jesus affect that goal?

**Note:** For next week's session, please bring along your current calendar or a to-do list for work, family, or both. It may be on your phone, written on a scrap of paper, or penciled into a planner or calendar. Whether high-tech, low-tech, or just in your head, be ready to share the means and method you use to organize your time.

*Closing Prayer*

> *Lord, help us to throw off all the stuff that bogs us down—the papers and books and toys and games and knickknacks and decorations and crafts and hobbies and memorabilia and gifts and souvenirs and fashions and records and all the other excess stuff we accumulate. We know that life does not consist of an abundance of possessions; rather, you and you alone are the way, the truth, and the life. So help us to order our homes in such a way that we can pursue an abundant life in you. Amen.*

# Personal Study

Dig deeper into the material covered in this week's video teaching by engaging in the following between-sessions activities. Be sure to make a few notes in your guide about the experience. There will be a time for you to share these reflections at the beginning of the next group session.

---

**Read and Reflect**
Matthew 13:12, 22, 44–45
Matthew 19:21

**Book Time**
For more inspiration and practical help, read chapters 1–3 of *Unstuffed*.

---

## Activity 1: Get FREE of Clutter

Before we get FREE of clutter, let's take a moment to examine the concept of freedom. One definition of freedom is "the state of being not imprisoned or enslaved."

➤ In what ways do your possessions enslave or imprison you?

➤ Where can you find freedom from your slavery? (See John 8:36; Acts 13:39; Romans 6:18.)

➤ Another definition of freedom is "the power to act without hindrance or restraint." What more could you accomplish for God's kingdom if you were free of clutter?

With Christ and the freedom he offers firmly in mind, let's follow Ruth's steps for decluttering. Make notes under the following points to remind yourself of your commitment to get **FREE** of clutter.

### F for Fight the Flow

Where do you need to stop visiting in order to stop bringing in more stuff?

➤ I need to avoid these stores:
- •
- •
- •

➤ I need to avoid and perhaps even block these websites:
- •
- •
- •

➤ I need to cancel these catalogs:

- 
- 
- 

➤ Looking at this list of places I need to avoid, I can tell that I most struggle with these heart issues:

- 
- 
- 

➤ With the help and guidance of the Holy Spirit, I pledge to fight my insecurities and compulsions, and to focus instead on the freedom offered to me in Jesus. I commit now to planning ahead and buying only essentials. Here is a list of essential items I will need in the next month (excluding groceries and gas for the car):

- 
- 
- 
- 
- 

## R for Ruthlessly Purge

Turn to Activity #1, "Deadly Greed," on pages 59–62. If you didn't tackle an area of clutter last week, try to do so this week. Take "before" and "after" photos and record here how it feels to declutter and organize. Did you strike a blow against greed? Are you feeling less anxious or depressed? Are you experiencing some of the freedom that Jesus promises when we put him first? How does that sense of freedom motivate you to do more purging?

*E for Establish Limits*

Think of three areas of your home, life, or heart where you want to enforce a limit. This could be your wardrobe, your hobby paraphernalia, your habit of always saying "yes," or your desire to make everyone happy, for example.

Write three limits here:

- 
- 
- 

Once you have the limit set, stick to it! And remember, as much as our society tells us otherwise, we already *have* enough (and in Christ, you already *are* enough!).

*E for Emphasize Quality*

➤ Determine one area where you want to choose quality over quantity. Define what quality means to you. Is it what something is made of or is it more geared toward where it is from, who made it, or what it represents? How might emphasizing quality in this area help you?

➤ In John 8:32 Jesus says, "Then you will know the truth, and the truth will set you free." What truth have you learned through this process? How has it set you free?

## Activity 2: The Proverbs 31 Woman

The "Proverbs 31 Woman" is generally regarded as an unattainable ideal. But without heroes and role models, how would we know what heights we are capable of achieving? Read these verses from Proverbs 31 and answer the questions, looking for areas where you might improve as well as areas you've mastered. Don't beat yourself up; simply try to target areas of concern, and then pray about them. And when you realize you are doing well in an area, thankfully accept the honor and praise that is your due! You deserve a gold star—and a ruby as well!

> [10]A wife of noble character who can find?
>     She is worth far more than rubies.

➤ **What does the state of your house say about your character?**

> [11]Her husband has full confidence in her
>     and lacks nothing of value.

➤ **Does your husband have confidence in your handling of your home? Is he lacking anything of value? Or if you are single, do you have full confidence in your abilities? Where could you improve?**

¹²She brings him good, not harm,
    all the days of her life.

➤ **What good are you bringing to your home and your relationships? How might you be harming them?**

¹³She selects wool and flax
    and works with eager hands.

➤ **How is your work ethic? Are you teaching your children the value of hard work by your example?**

¹⁴She is like the merchant ships,
    bringing her food from afar.
¹⁵She gets up while it is still night;
    she provides food for her family
    and portions for her female servants.

➤ **Are you working hard to feed yourself and your family nourishing meals? Do you treat your employees and colleagues with respect?**

[16]She considers a field and buys it;

out of her earnings she plants a vineyard.

[17]She sets about her work vigorously;

her arms are strong for her tasks.

[18]She sees that her trading is profitable,

and her lamp does not go out at night.

[19]In her hand she holds the distaff

and grasps the spindle with her fingers.

➤ Are you planning ahead financially? Are you working vigorously to improve your profits?

[20]She opens her arms to the poor

and extends her hands to the needy.

➤ Are you generous in sharing your time and treasure?

[21]When it snows, she has no fear for her household;

for all of them are clothed in scarlet.

[22]She makes coverings for her bed;

she is clothed in fine linen and purple.

➤ Are you prepared for emergencies? Are you and your family neatly clothed and your home cared for?

[25]She is clothed with strength and dignity;
    she can laugh at the days to come.

➤ **Can you face the future with strength, dignity, and humor?**

[26]She speaks with wisdom,
    and faithful instruction is on her tongue.

➤ **Are you faithfully teaching your children how to live according to God's Word?**

[27]She watches over the affairs of her household
    and does not eat the bread of idleness.

➤ **Are you watching over your household, making sure each family member is cared for physically, emotionally, and spiritually? Or do you spend too much time on social media, shopping, and binge-watching TV?**

> [28] Her children arise and call her blessed;
>    her husband also, and he praises her:
> [29] "Many women do noble things,
>    but you surpass them all."

➤ **Are your family relationships for the most part encouraging and harmonious?**

> [30] Charm is deceptive, and beauty is fleeting;
>    but a woman who fears the LORD is to be praised.

➤ **Which do you value more and spend the most time on—your accomplishments, popularity, and physical appearance or your character and relationship with God?**

> [31] Honor her for all that her hands have done,
>    and let her works bring her praise at the city gate.

➤ **Do these verses help you realize how important it is to care for your home and family? How does that motivate you in your battle against stuff?**

## Activity 3: Conclusion and Reflection

Matthew 6:21 says, "For where your treasure is, there your heart will be also." Our possessions inevitably reveal our priorities. Ask yourself: Are my priorities on track (heavenly) or out of whack (earthly)? Take a spiritual inventory of your possessions, including the blessings of any extra money and leisure time. Ask yourself the following questions and write honest answers.

### My Home

➤ Why do I live where I do? How does my home help or hinder my walk with God?

### My Clothing

➤ What kind of clothing do I buy? Why? How do my clothing choices and buying habits help or hinder my walk with God?

### My Furniture and Household Goods

➤ How do I furnish and decorate my home? Why? How do those choices help or hinder my walk with God?

*My Car*

➤ What kind of car do I drive? Why? How does this choice help or hinder my walk with God?

*My Food*

➤ What kind of food do I buy? Why? How does this choice help or hinder my walk with God?

*My Extra Money*

➤ Where do I spend any extra money I may have? Why? How does this choice help or hinder my walk with God?

*My Vacations*

➤ What kind of vacations do I take? Why? How does this choice help or hinder my walk with God?

Use the space below to write any key points, realizations, or questions you want to bring to the next group meeting. In addition, for next week's lesson, don't forget to bring along your current calendar or to-do list for work, family, or both.

# Mind

A busy life is not the same as a
meaningful, obedient one.

## Opening Reflection (5 MINUTES)

Spend some time sharing your thoughts and reflections from last week's session or personal study. Is there an experience or realization that stood out to you? Did you make progress in some area?

## Session Introduction (5 MINUTES)

Our culture not only embraces a go-go-go mentality but perpetuates it. The underlying message is that if our lives aren't completely full, they don't count. And it's not just *our* lives; it's our kids' lives as well. The main problem in this culture of busy is the fear that we might miss out, or worse, a fear that our kids might fall behind. Without really intending it to happen, the busyness becomes our first priority, the thing we value above all else. The busyness becomes our idol.

- List at least three "busy things" that take up your time but don't seem meaningful, necessary, or done in obedience to God's plan for you. Then share at least one of your answers with the group.
    1.
    2.
    3.

## Watch the Video (14 MINUTES)

*Play the* Unstuffed *video segment titled "Mind." As you watch, fill in the blanks in the following outline to help you recall the main concepts presented.*

How much is too much? How long can my _____ list become before it overwhelms me?

A busy life is not the same as a _____ one.

Jesus says in Matthew 11:28, "Come to me, all you who are _____ and burdened, and I will give you rest."

Rest has been with us from the very beginning of time: "By the seventh day God had finished the work he had been doing; so on the seventh day he _____ from all his work. Then God blessed the seventh day and made it holy, because on it he rested from all the work of creating that he had done." (Genesis 2:2–3)

Here are a few concrete strategies that might help you break free of the guilt that is paralyzing you and finally help you get rid of all those items you've been hanging on to:

> First, change the _____.
> Second, decide to _____.
> Next, set _____ before you begin.
> Last, do it _____.

---

**Fill-in answers (in order):** to-do, meaningful, weary, rested, tape, decide, limits, scared

---

## Opening Prayer

*Lord Jesus, we are drowning in the sea of our self-inflicted busyness. Yes, we need to work; yes, we need to care for our families; yes, we want to help out at church and at school and in our community; but Lord, when do we stop? When do we say no? When do we get a chance to rest? Thank you, Jesus, for reminding us that your yoke is easy and your burden is light. You didn't make us for meaningless activity but for obedient, meaningful lives characterized by a rhythm of productive work and restorative rest. Help us to fear missing out not on the next activity but on your grace. Amen.*

## Icebreaker: Check Your Calendar! (10 MINUTES)

Last week we asked you to bring along your calendar or to-do list for work or home. Take it out now for a bit of show-and-tell. If you have a large group, break into a smaller group of three or four people. Show the group your method for handling your schedule or your to-do list. Then discuss a few of these questions:

- What do you like about your method? Would you recommend it to others?
- What method have you tried in the past that did not work for you?
- How do you choose what goes on your calendar or to-do list (are you mainly reactive or proactive; do you pray about it)?
- What one thing could you delete from your calendar or to-do list?
- What does your calendar or to-do list reveal about your priorities? Are you happy with those priorities, or do they need adjusting?

## Group Discussion (25 MINUTES)

*Read the following passage:*

> Come to me, all you who are weary and burdened, and I will give you rest. Take my yoke upon you and learn from me, for I am gentle and humble in heart, and you will find rest for your souls. For my yoke is easy and my burden is light (Matthew 11:28–30).

1. What portion of these verses spoke to you most? Why?

2. Sometimes the Christian life can seem anything but easy! If Jesus' yoke doesn't seem easy or light, what does that say about how we are living the Christian life? What might we be doing wrong?

*Read the following passage:*

> [Jesus said], "I have told you these things, so that in me you may have peace. In this world you will have trouble. But take heart! I have overcome the world" (John 16:33).

3. How does it help you to know that Jesus has "overcome the world" and its troubles, which include your busyness, your to-do list, and your crazy calendar of commitments?

Jesus and his followers were busy teaching, healing, and traveling from place to place, sharing the good news. But Jesus asked them to do just so much—and no more.

*Read the following passage:*

> The apostles gathered around Jesus and reported to him all they had done and taught. Then, because so many people were coming and going that they did not even have a chance to eat, he said to them, "Come with me by yourselves to a quiet place and get some rest." So they went away by themselves in a boat to a solitary place (Mark 6:30–32).

4. What does this passage teach you about the importance of caring for your own needs?

5. Why is it important to get away from the crowds and busyness to spend time alone?

6. Share the story of a time when you or someone else suffered because you did not take the time to care for yourself. What did you learn from that experience?

*Read the following passage:*

> By the seventh day God had finished the work he had been doing; so on the seventh day he rested from all his work. Then God blessed the seventh day and made it holy, because on it he rested from all the work of creating that he had done (Genesis 2:2–3).

7. Do you make a point of keeping a day of rest? If so, how do you prepare for and partake of that rest? What is the result?

If not, why are you not able to take a day of rest? Is there another way you could incorporate rest into your life?

### Closing Prayer

*Lord, thank you for recognizing that we are weary and burdened from way too much stuff and way too much to do. Help us to learn from you how to rest—to take one day a week, one hour a day, even one minute an hour    to refocus on you. Thank you for the gift and blessing of a day of rest, a reminder that we don't need to be slaves to our schedules but are instead beloved children of our heavenly Father, invited to relax and play in this beautiful world you've given us. As we examine our schedules, to-do lists, and precious family heirlooms, help us to make choices about our time and treasure that honor and serve you above all. Amen.*

# Personal Study

Dig deeper into the material covered in this week's video teaching by engaging in the following between-sessions activities. Be sure to make a few notes in your guide about the experience. There will be a time for you to share these reflections at the beginning of the next group session.

---

**Read and Reflect**
Ecclesiastes 3:1–15
Matthew 24:36–51

**Book Time**
For more inspiration and practical help, read chapters 4–6 of *Unstuffed*.

---

## Activity 1: Spiritual Inventory

We will spend some time next week talking about the importance of rest and downtime. For now, let's take a spiritual inventory of the ways we keep ourselves busy. Matthew 6:21 says, "For where your treasure is, there your heart will be also." Or to paraphrase, "For where we spend our time, there our heart will be also." Our schedules inevitably reveal our priorities. Ask yourself: Are my priorities on track (heavenly) or out of whack (earthly)? Get out your calendar and take a spiritual inventory of your schedule. Ask yourself the following questions and write honest answers.

*My Paid or Volunteer Work*

(inside or outside the home, including commute)

➤ Approximate hours worked per week: _____

➤ Why do I work as much as I do? How does my work outside the home help or hinder my walk with God and relationships with others?

*My Work at Home*

➤ Approximate hours worked per week: _____

➤ Do I spend too much time or not enough time caring for my household needs (including shopping, cooking, cleaning, childcare, etc.)? How do my choices help or hinder my walk with God and my relationships with others?

*My Close Relationships*

➤ Approximate hours worked per week: _____

➤ Do I build in daily and weekly time to spend with my spouse, children, or friends? How do those choices help or hinder my walk with God?

*My School and/or Community*

➤ Approximate hours worked per week: _____

➤ Do I spend too much or too little time helping others? How do those choices help or hinder my walk with God?

*My Church*

➤ Approximate hours worked per week: _____

➤ Do I spend enough time worshiping, volunteering, and building community? How do those choices help or hinder my walk with God?

*My Self-Care*
(including sleep, grooming, and exercise)

➤ Approximate hours worked per week: _____

➤ Do I spend too much or too little time caring for myself? How do those choices help or hinder my walk with God?

*My Leisure Time*

(including TV, surfing the internet, gaming, hobbies, reading, shopping for pleasure, etc.)

➤ Approximate hours worked per week: _____

➤ Do I spend too much or too little time enjoying leisure? How do those choices help or hinder my walk with God and relationships with others?

*My Time with God*

➤ Approximate hours worked per week: _____

➤ Do I spend time with God? Do I keep him in my thoughts as I go through my daily activities, and do I live my life to obey and glorify him or to satisfy myself?

➤ Having taken inventory of how you spend your time, what area stands out as a red flag?

Paul reminds us, "The time is short. . . . This world in its present form is passing away. [Therefore] those who use the things of the world [should use them] as if not engrossed in them" (1 Corinthians 7:29, 31b, 31a). In light of eternity, are you too engrossed in the things of this world?

➤ What one change can you make to your schedule that will reflect kingdom priorities instead of worldly priorities? Pray about it, and then ask the Holy Spirit to help you make that change.

## Activity 2: Guilt and Stuff

We want to be free of the clutter in our homes, but we are just as desperate to be free of the weight of the guilt attached to all these items. As humans, we have plenty to feel guilty about. As Romans 3:23 puts it, "For all have sinned and fall short of the glory of God." Thankfully, though, there is a cure for that guilt: "All are justified freely by his grace through the redemption that came by Christ Jesus" (Romans 3:24).

➤ Sometimes decluttering involves disposing of cherished gifts and heirlooms. How does the knowledge of God's grace help you to deal not only with the guilt of your sin but also more specifically with the guilt of discarding items associated with a loved one?

*Read Luke 12:13–21. Then answer the following questions.*

➤ What will happen to *your* stuff when you die? Are you conscious of how disposing of your possessions will affect your loved ones?

➤ If you've received something from someone who has passed away, was that inheritance a gift or a burden?

➤ What do you want *your* legacy to be?

➤ Paul reminds us in 2 Corinthians 5:17 that "the old has gone, the new is here!" How does your new life in Christ help to remind you of what really matters?

With God's grace and your new life in Christ firmly in mind, find an item that you have had difficulty discarding. Then "change the tape" by switching out the guilt message that plays over and over in your brain. Pinpoint your own personal guilt trap regarding that item, and then highlight the "tape" below that you need to play instead:

| Guilt Trap | Internal Message | New Message |
|---|---|---|
| Worried about feeling wasteful | "But I might use this someday." | Someone else can use it right now. |
| Financial guilt | "But I spent good money on that." | The money is already gone. Better to sell it and recoup some of the loss. |
| Sentimental guilt | "But it means so much!" | Take a picture. Memories and objects are not the same thing. |
| Hurting some-one's feelings | "But it was a gift!" | Thank the giver, and you are free to find a new home for the gift. |

*cont.*

| Guilt Trap | Internal Message | New Message |
|---|---|---|
| Haven't reached a goal | "But I might finish that someday." | Sometimes it is okay to fail so I can focus on other priorities and opportunities. |
| Parental guilt | "But I just want my kids to be happy!" | Too much stuff creates discontented and spoiled kids. |
| Memory guilt | "But I'm throwing away their memory!" | Don't equate a loved one with the stuff they left behind. |

If possible, hold the item in your hand. If you are still feeling guilty about disposing of this item, decide to decide. In other words: just do it. Discard or donate it *now*, and do it scared. Then report back to the group session next week for accountability (and to inspire others to do the same!).

In the end, learning to give up the guilt we've attached to so much of the stuff filling up our lives is a lifelong process. But as we keep working at it, we will find a life that is so much freer than we ever thought possible.

## Activity 3: Conclusion and Reflection

In his book *Counterfeit Gods*, pastor Timothy Keller points out that nearly anything and everything can become an idol in our lives—something we prioritize, love, trust, and even obey in place of God. In the process of decluttering our homes and schedules, we might have uncovered the things we have been valuing above all else—things like a nice home, our kids, a successful career, an elevated social status, or even things that are less tangible, like feeling good about ourselves, feeling productive, or simply wanting to be happy.

But with all of these pursuits, despite how important and valuable they might appear to be, we will inevitably find that something is still missing. After all, what happens when happiness fails us? When our social status crumbles? When our kids let us down? Or when our job is downsized? We may declutter our homes, unstuff our schedules, and destress our lives, sweeping them clean, putting them in order, but what then? Who—or what—will fill that space?

➤ Read Matthew 12:43–45. What will fill the swept-clean spaces in your life if you're not careful?

➤ Read Exodus 20:1–3. Why do you think God made this the first of the Ten Commandments?

➤ What does this tell you about how God expects us to fill our hearts and lives?

Read Matthew 6:24: "No one can serve two masters. Either you will hate the one and love the other, or you will be devoted to the one and despise the other. You cannot serve both God and money."

Take the word *money* in the above passage and substitute one of the following words that best describes your current idol:

- Fame
- Success
- My kids
- My spouse
- My job
- Beauty
- Comfort
- Security
- Control
- Social status
- Happiness
- Busyness

➤ Why can't you serve both God and that particular idol?

➤ Read Matthew 6:33. How can you seek Jesus' kingdom first **today**? Pray and ask Jesus to show you what to prioritize today.

Use the space below to write any key points, realizations, or questions you want to bring to the next group meeting.

# Soul

---

**What if we took the time to rest, rejuvenate, and cultivate real relationships with God and others?**

---

## Opening Reflection (5 MINUTES)

Spend some time sharing your thoughts and reflections from last week's session or personal study. Is there an experience or realization that stood out to you? Did you make progress in some area?

## Session Introduction (5 MINUTES)

In this time of virtual reality and social media "friends" who are not really friends, we need to relearn the art of cultivating real relationships. True friends nourish and strengthen us. Virtual friends inflame our envy and resentment. True friends are honest. Virtual friends hide behind carefully edited photos and posts. True friends help us feel desired and included. Virtual friends often make us feel like we are missing out.

Take a moment to think about the following questions, and then have three to five people share their FOMO (fear of missing out) stories with the group.

- When is the last time you experienced FOMO, the fear of missing out? What did you do about it? Was your response helpful or hurtful?

## Watch the Video (20 MINUTES)

*Play the* Unstuffed *video segment titled "Soul." As you watch, fill in the blanks in the following outline to help you recall the main concepts presented.*

We often base our relationships on what we think we can get out of the relationship rather than what we are willing to _____.

Paul writes in 1 Corinthians 13:4–8: "Love is patient, love is _____.
It does not envy, it does not boast, it is not proud. It does not dishonor
others, it is not self-seeking, it is not easily angered, it keeps no record
of wrongs. Love does not delight in evil but rejoices with the truth.
It always protects, always trusts, always hopes, always perseveres.
Love never _____."

When it comes to real relationships, the ability to forgive and forget is not
just important; it is _____.

Balance in our day-to-day lives really can only happen once we are willing to
stop _____ and start _____.

How do we learn to relax, especially if we're not really wired that way? I have
found the following strategies to be helpful:

Keep your weekends _____.
Let go of the _____.
Give yourself _____.

---

**Fill-in answers (in order):** put into it, kind, fails, essential, doing,
resting, free, FOMO, grace

---

*Opening Prayer*

*Lord Jesus, we long to have good friends and to be a good friend, yet so
often busyness gets in the way, and we find it easier to be superficial than
to dig deep, to hide behind Facebook posts instead of meeting face-to-face.
Help us to find balance in our chaotic world, to get enough rest, exercise,
and downtime that we have the resources to invest in the most precious
gift you've given us: our relationships with loved ones. And, Lord, help
us to deepen our relationship with you as well. Amen.*

## Icebreaker: Loving (and Losing) Friends (10 MINUTES)

In the chart below, list your current closest friends as well as friends you have lost. Then take a few minutes to share with the group your answer to one of these questions: What qualities do you value in one of your closest friends? What caused you to lose a past friendship?

| Current Close Friends | Friends I've Lost |
| --- | --- |
|  |  |

## Group Discussion (20 MINUTES)

*Read this passage:*

> Love is patient, love is kind. It does not envy, it does not boast, it is not proud. It does not dishonor others, it is not self-seeking, it is not easily angered, it keeps no record of wrongs. Love does not delight in evil but rejoices with the truth. It always protects, always trusts, always hopes, always perseveres. Love never fails. . . . And now these three remain: faith, hope and love. But the greatest of these is love (1 Corinthians 13:4–8, 13).

1. Think of a person you know who exemplifies this kind of love. What specifically do they do to demonstrate love, and how do you respond to it? Share a brief description or story of this person with the group.

A 1 Corinthians 13 type of love could also be known as *selflessness*. Now read this "reverse" 1 Corinthians 13, describing *selfishness*:

> Selfishness is impatient and unkind; a self-centered heart is full of envy and boasting; self-centeredness reveals itself in arrogance and rudeness. Selfishness insists on its own way; a self-centered mind will lead me to be irritable and resentful; self-centeredness has no qualms about celebrating sin or mocking what is true. Selfishness is whiny and thin-skinned; a self-centered spirit provokes me to be thoroughly skeptical, always pessimistic, and consistently willing to give up, give in, and walk away from what matters most. Selfishness will be brought to a shameful, disgraceful end. . . . For now, pettiness, bitterness, and hatred abide in this world; but the temporary root of all of this rotten fruit is selfishness (1 Worldliness 13).*

2. We've all experienced times when our own selfishness reared its ugly head. How does this selfishness affect our relationships? How does it affect our emotions and attitudes? How does it affect our walk with God?

3. To be real, we often find that certain people bring out the best in us, while others seem to elicit the worst. Think of someone who brings out the best in you. What is it about this person that makes you a better person? Have a few people in the group share their answers.

---

* Jason Hardin, In God's Image, sermon, "1 Corinthians in Reverse" (September 19, 2014), http://www .ingodsimage.com/2014/09/1-corinthians-13-in-reverse/.

4. Think of someone who sometimes brings out the worst in you. What is it about this person that rubs you the wrong way or makes you behave in a way you are ashamed of? Why do you think this happens? Have a few people in the group share their answers.

*Read this passage:*

> Then Peter came to Jesus and asked, "Lord, how many times shall I forgive my brother or sister who sins against me? Up to seven times?" Jesus answered, "I tell you, not seven times, but seventy-seven times" (Matthew 18:21–22).

5. Here's a thought: Often the person who brings out the best in us is the same as the person who brings out the worst in us! (Hint: think spouse, child, or someone close enough to us to encounter our flaws.) How does "seventy-seven times" forgiveness enable us to restore and repair those important relationships?

6. Read 1 John 1:9. How does confessing our sins to Jesus help us to deal with our guilt and shame?

### Closing Prayer

*Lord, our relationships are the most precious thing in our lives, yet it's so easy to damage them with neglect and selfishness. Fill our hearts with your ridiculously unimaginable, perfect, eternal love, a love described in that best and most eloquent of all love poems, 1 Corinthians 13. Make us patient, kind, humble, trustworthy, hopeful, and persevering. Lord, your love will never fail us. Help us cling to you, the Source and Spirit of Love. Amen.*

# Personal Study

Dig deeper into the material covered in this week's video teaching by engaging in the following between-sessions activities. Be sure to make a few notes in your guide about the experience. There will be a time for you to share these reflections at the beginning of the next group session.

---

### Read and Reflect
1 Samuel 20
Proverbs 12:26; 17:9; 18:24

### Book Time
For more inspiration and practical help, read chapters 7–8 of *Unstuffed*.

---

## Activity 1: 1 Corinthians 13 Love

Continue using 1 Corinthians 13 to dig into these probing questions. Note areas of concern and pray about them.

- *Love is patient.* In an increasingly fast-paced world, it's difficult to make time for relationships. Am I intentionally carving out time in my schedule to nurture my important relationships?

- *Love is kind.* We should always treat each other with respect. Do I build up my friends and family members rather than tear them down? Am I slow to criticize? Do I choose my words carefully? Am I nice?

- *Love does not envy.* Have I recently come face-to-face with the green-eyed monster? Is deep-seated discontentment clouding my view of the people I love?

- *Love is not proud.* Do I spend a lot of time posting carefully curated photos on Facebook and Pinterest? Do I toot my own horn or try to build myself up in front of others? Am I quick to bring attention to myself, or do I turn the focus to others?

- *Love rejoices with the truth.* Real relationships are honest, even when honesty is hard. Am I a truth teller in my relationships, or do I skate over facts in favor of what is easy or pleasant?

- *Love is not self-seeking.* Are my relationships all about me—my feelings, desires, and needs? Or do I put my friend's needs ahead of my own?

- *Love is not easily angered. Love keeps no record of wrongs.* Am I quick to judge or become annoyed, or am I willing to give people the benefit of the doubt, even when they've done something to offend me?

- *Love always protects.* Do I look out for my friends and do what I can to keep them safe from harm? Am I willing to jump in and defend them against attack? Do I protect and shelter the people I love?

- *Love always trusts.* Do I deserve the trust and confidence of others? Do I live my life with integrity? Am I dependable and reliable? Do I avoid gossiping and talking about others? Do I keep my promises?

- *Love never fails.* Am I committed to my relationships? Am I in it for the long haul, even when things get hard?

## Activity 2: Made to Rest

God built rest right into the structure of creation; after he finished creating the world, he rested (Genesis 2:2).

➤ Why do you think rest is so important? What does the institution of rest show us about God?

➤ God reemphasized the importance of rest when he gave his chosen people the Ten Commandments. Read Exodus 20:8. Who and what were commanded to rest? Why was God so detailed in his instructions here?

➤ God believed a day of rest was so important that he commanded it and blessed it and called it holy. Do you observe a day of rest? Why or why not? What do you need to do to set aside time that is a restful blessing, a time that is special and honors God and others?

The opposite of rest is restlessness. Not only does the Bible show us the importance of rest and the blessings we enjoy when we obey God's command to rest, but it also reveals that the result of disobedience and estrangement from God is restlessness.

➤ Read the story of Cain and Abel in Genesis 4. What is the result of Cain's sin (vv. 12–14)?

➤ Read Proverbs 4:14–17, especially verse 16. How is the wicked person described?

➤ Jesus also emphasized the importance of rest. Read Matthew 11:28–29. How would you describe what Jesus means by "rest for your soul"? What does that phrase mean to you?

➤ Like us, Jesus worked hard, but he recognized the need for space and quiet after times of busyness and stress. Read Mark 6:31. Have you ever been so busy that you neglected your own needs, even your need for food and sleep? What is Jesus' prescription for you?

Do you need to relearn how to rest? Try one of the following activities and record your impressions about the experience. As you relax, reflect and give thanks for God's good gift of rest.

- Take one day off. Consciously and purposefully set aside one day solely for rest and relaxation.
- Unplug. Set aside screen-free time in your day to allow yourself time away from the constant stream of connectivity.
- Take a nap. Research has shown again and again the effectiveness of taking a short power nap during the day. A short nap can recharge your brain and make you more productive.
- Spend time outside. There is something almost magical about getting outside in the fresh air, even if just for a few minutes.

- Discover what relaxes you—and do it. For different people, this will mean different things. Don't feel as though you need to adopt someone else's idea of relaxation; figure out what works best for you.
- Keep your weekend free. Instead of going out, consciously plan to do nothing but stay at home and enjoy your loved ones.

## Activity 3: Conclusion and Reflection

In his ministry, Jesus prioritized relationships. One of the first things he did was to choose twelve men who would live with him, travel with him, learn from him, minister with him, and pray with him. They were not only his disciples; they were his friends.

*Read John 15:9–17.*

➤ **What are the primary characteristics of Jesus' relationship with his disciples, including us?**

➤ **How does he demonstrate his love for us?**

➤ How can we, in turn, demonstrate our love for him?

It takes effort and intention to be a good friend, and to cultivate real relationships in your life. Let's learn from Jesus the principles of how to make a lasting friendship:

1. *Take the initiative.* Jesus didn't wait for people to come to him; he reached out to them first (Matthew 4:18–22). There is no reason to sit around waiting for someone else to make the first move. The same goes for the friends you already have—you must nurture those friendships or they will wither and die. It takes very little effort to send out a quick text message every now and then. At the very least, start there.

2. *Be intentional.* Jesus chose twelve men—no more, no less—because he knew the number of disciples he needed to accomplish his mission on earth. A big part of taking the initiative to improve your relationships means taking the time to be intentional about who you are reaching out to. Don't pursue too many friendships—remember, this is about quality, not quantity.

3. *Prioritize face-to-face friendships.* Jesus chose friends with whom he could share his daily life. Sometimes we can spend so much energy investing in old friends or acquaintances via Facebook that we neglect real friendships we could make or deepen in real life right now. Make an effort to spend less time online and more time chatting with the people in your face-to-face world.

4. *Listen.* Jesus was alert and aware of what his friends were thinking, discussing, and doing (see, for example, Matthew 16:5–8; Mark 10:35–45; Matthew 26:36–46). In contrast, much of social media is about putting your own life on display, hoping to elicit a response. So turn this dynamic on its head. Instead of being eager to share your own trials, tribulations, and triumphs, try focusing on the person you are connecting with.

5. *Pray.* Jesus prayed for his disciples and continues to pray for us (John 17:6–25). Nothing changes the way we feel about someone or makes us care for them more deeply than praying for them regularly.

6. *Go deep.* Jesus was willing to confront, challenge, and question his friends (see, for example, John 13:6–9, 18–30; 18:10–11). Be willing to talk about the hard stuff with your friends, both in your life and in theirs.

7. *Make time for friendship.* Remember the most basic rule of friendship? In order to have a friend, you must be a friend. In order to be our friend, Jesus left his heavenly throne and became one of us—born as a helpless baby, he grew up just like us, and experienced all the trials and temptations that we encounter. What a friend! Take a moment right now to thank Jesus for his friendship.

Now make a short list of people with whom you'd like to cultivate a real relationship. Put an action plan in place to make it happen! Send a text asking for prayer requests or invite them out to coffee. Be intentional and reserve time to allow your friendships to flourish.

*Future Friendship #1*

**Who:** I would like to cultivate a relationship with . . .

**How:** I will do that by . . .

**When:** And here's the date or time I'll do that . . .

*Future Friendship #2*

**Who:** I would like to cultivate a relationship with . . .

**How:** I will do that by . . .

**When:** And here's the date or time I'll do that . . .

*Future Friendship #3*

**Who:** I would like to cultivate a relationship with . . .

**How:** I will do that by . . .

**When:** And here's the date or time I'll do that . . .

Use the space below to write any key points, realizations, or questions you want to bring to the next group meeting.

# Unstuffed for Good

The only way to deal with our messes is to recognize that God has already wiped our slate clean.

## Opening Reflection (5 MINUTES)

Spend some time sharing your thoughts and reflections from last week's session or personal study. Is there an experience or realization that stood out to you? Did you make progress in some area?

## Session Introduction (5 MINUTES)

Learning how to stop the incoming flow of stuff in our lives, learning how to ruthlessly purge and set limits, learning how to find balance in the midst of a hectic schedule, learning how to nurture real relationships and take the time to rest—all of those things are valuable lessons worth learning and refining and striving for. But in the end, if we are trying to do all of these things simply to save ourselves, we are doomed to fail. The only way to become and stay unstuffed is to accept the amazing grace we've already been given.

- We've learned a lot over the last weeks and been challenged to change many assumptions and behaviors. Take a few minutes and share one "aha" moment you experienced or one change you made as a result of taking part in this group study.

## Watch the Video (22 MINUTES)

*Play the* Unstuffed *video segment titled "Unstuffed for Good." As you watch, fill in the blanks in the following outline to help you recall the main concepts presented. Because this video contains little to no onscreen text, you will need to listen carefully for the missing words or discern them from the context. (As usual, the answer key follows these notes.)*

Ruth prayed and discovered amazing _____ even for a train wreck like her.

One of the biggest problems we face is the idea that once we have been saved, we are somehow "_____."

Three people who also "messed up": _____, _____, and _____.

Romans 7:18–19: "For I know that _____ itself does not dwell in me, that is, in my sinful nature. For I have the desire to do what is good, but I cannot carry it out. For I do not do the good I want to do, but the evil I do not want to do—this I keep on doing."

Truly unstuffed = _____ the grace we've been given and stop trying to fill that hole ourselves.

God loves us not because we are _____ but because he is.

---

**Fill-in answers (in order):** grace, fixed, David, Peter, Paul, good, accept, perfect

---

*Opening Prayer*

> *Lord Jesus, over the past few weeks, we've had to come face-to-face with our own messes. Sometimes the mess is in our homes; other times it's in our hearts. Help us to hand our messes over to you, knowing that you have already done the hard work of cleaning us up. Thank you for loving and using messed-up, flawed, not-good-enough people like us. Help us to keep trusting in your amazing grace to save and sanctify us. Amen.*

## Icebreaker: Messed Up (10 minutes)

If you are willing, share one area where you feel you are currently "messed up" or where you have messed up in the past. How have you handled that failure? What do you wish you could have done differently?

Or here's another way of looking at that question. In what ways have you tried to save yourself? What were the results?

## Group Discussion (20 MINUTES)

1. We have lots of different ways of messing up—some obvious, others less so. Take a moment to read the list below on your own, marking places where you're currently messed up or you've messed up in the past:
   - ☐ Shopping too much
   - ☐ Piling up credit card debt
   - ☐ Overscheduling and overcommitting
   - ☐ Procrastinating or being lazy
   - ☐ Being bitter and angry
   - ☐ Leading a double life
   - ☐ Making an idol out of my spouse, kids, home, or job
   - ☐ Being addicted to drugs, alcohol, romance, attention, affirmation, popularity, achievement
   - ☐ Living with subtle messes: dirty house, late bills, too little time and energy to do what really matters

2. No matter what your mess is, here is a truth. In John 10:10, Jesus says, "I am the gate; whoever enters through me will be saved. They will come in and go out, and find pasture. The thief comes only to steal and kill and destroy; I have come that they may have life, and have it to the full." Or, in the words of the New Living Translation: "My [Jesus'] purpose is to give them a rich and satisfying life."

   How does our society's definition of a rich and satisfying life differ from Jesus' definition of the full life?

3. Why are we so drawn to society's definition of the full life?

4. Why is that definition incomplete and ultimately unsatisfying?

5. In light of all we've learned over the course of this study, can we recalibrate our desires and focus on where Jesus points us?

*Now read Paul's lament:*

> For I know that good itself does not dwell in me, that is, in my sinful nature. For I have the desire to do what is good, but I cannot carry it out. For I do not do the good I want to do, but the evil I do not want to do—this I keep on doing (Romans 7:18-19).

*Now read:*

> And what is Paul's answer to our dilemma? Is it shame? Is it hopelessness? No! Hear this: "Therefore, there is now no condemnation for those who are in Christ Jesus, because through Christ Jesus the law of the Spirit who gives life has set you free from the law of sin and death" (Romans 8:1-2).

6. How does knowing that you are not condemned for what you've done (or left undone) help you?

### Closing Prayer

*Lord, if we would only trust you and ask, you could set us free of our guilt, shame, and insecurity. We've tried so hard, but we've found out that we are simply unable to save ourselves. Save us, we beg you! Save us from our unbelief, skepticism, and cynicism, which keep us from trusting you. Save us from our self-righteousness and perfectionism, which keep us frantically trying to earn the grace you've already given us. Save us from ourselves, Jesus. You made us. You love us. Now keep us in your care. Amen.*

# Personal Study

Dig deeper into the material covered in this week's video teaching by engaging in the following activities.

---

**Read and Reflect**
Romans 3:23; 5:8; 6:23; 10:9-10, 13

**Book Time**
For more inspiration and practical help, read chapter 9 of *Unstuffed*.

---

## Activity 1: The Bigger Picture

In the video, Ruth shared much of her life story and concluded: "All these events in my life, all these things that had, up until that point, seemed random and unrelated, now made sense. It was like I had been standing right in front of a giant tapestry, staring so closely at one small section that I couldn't see the large picture. God pulled me back so I could see the whole thing, and it was far, far more beautiful than I could've ever imagined."

➤ Reflecting on your own life, are you currently staring closely at one small section? What is it? Why are you obsessing over that piece?

➤ If you could pull back, what might you see? What do you think God did to lead you to this point? What do you think he might be doing right now?

➤ If you are not able to pull back or to see any pattern in the events of your life, are you still willing to trust God's plan for you?

➤ The prophet Jeremiah wrote, "'For I know the plans I have for you,' declares the LORD, 'plans to prosper you and not to harm you, plans to give you hope and a future'" (Jeremiah 29:11). What do *you* think you need to prosper at this time? What might *God* think you need so you can prosper for eternity?

➤ David wrote, "Your eyes saw my unformed body; all the days ordained for me were written in your book before one of them came to be" (Psalm 139:16). How does it help you to know that God wrote the story of your life?

## Activity 2: Fatal Flaws

The Bible makes abundantly clear that God uses the most messed-up, flawed, not-good-enough people to do his will because messed-up, flawed, not-good-enough people are, quite frankly, all he has to choose from. Ruth already pointed out the flaws of three great heroes of the faith: David, Peter, and Paul. Let's look at a few other biblical "heroes." Read the following passages and answer the questions.

*Eve (**Genesis 3:1–7; 20**)*

Her fatal flaw:

How God used her:

*Sarah (**Genesis 16:1–6; 18:9–15; 21:1–13**)*

Her fatal flaw:

How God used her:

*Jonah (Jonah 1:1–12; 4:1–11)*

His fatal flaw:

How God used him:

*Take a moment to reflect on these questions:*

➤ **What is your fatal flaw?**

➤ **How might God be using you in spite of or even *because of* that flaw?**

## Activity 3: Conclusion and Reflection

We live in a do-it-yourself world, one that tells us again and again that if we can just try a little harder, do a little more, be a little better, we might just save ourselves. It is the same mentality that compels us to fill up our homes with stuff in the first place, because that stuff becomes the status symbol for the life we think we want. It is the same mentality that drives us to fill up our schedules, causing us to confuse busyness with meaning. We've stuffed ourselves to overflowing with the pressure to achieve. But it doesn't have to be that way.

In the end, salvation starts and ends with grace. The only way to become truly unstuffed is to accept the amazing, incredible, unlimited, and totally undeserved grace we've already been given and to stop trying to fill that hole ourselves. Grace is the answer we are often too stubborn to believe and too proud to receive.

Pray the following prayer. It might start out hesitantly; you might have to repeat it over and over again until it is true. But as you begin to unstuff your life, let God lead you, and embrace the plans he has for you right now, in this season of life.

*Jesus, I am no longer my own, but yours and yours alone. Use me for whatever you will, place me with whomever you will. Appoint me to do whatever you want, or to suffer whatever you ask. Let me be employed wherever, set aside whenever, lifted up however, or humbled forever. Let me be full, let me be empty, let me have whatever, or nothing whatsoever. I freely and willingly surrender whatsoever I have or am to your pleasure and will. And now, awesome and loving God, Father, Son, and Holy Spirit, you are mine and I am yours—whatever! And may this vow, which I have taken here on earth, sound loud and clear until there echoes through heaven the sound of your "Amen!"*

*Wesley Covenant Prayer*

# Additional Resources for Group Leaders

Thank you for your willingness to lead a group through *Living Well Spending Less/Unstuffed*! This eight-session study is built around video content and small-group interaction. As the group leader, your job is to take care of your group by managing all the behind-the-scenes details so that the group members can focus on interacting with one another and the topic. Your role is not to answer all the questions or reteach the content—the videos, books, and study guide will do most of that work. Your job is to guide the experience and cultivate your small group into a caring community where they can process, question, connect, and reflect on the material.

## Before You Begin

Before your first meeting, make sure the group members have a copy of this study guide. Alternately, you can hand out the study guides at your first meeting and give the group members some time to look over the material and ask any preliminary questions. While the books *Living Well Spending Less* and *Unstuffed* are not necessary for completing this study, you may encourage group members to purchase and read them for further inspiration, insight, and practical tips.

During your first meeting, send a sheet around the room and have each member write down her contact information. Generally, the ideal size for a group is between eight to ten people, which ensures everyone will have enough time to participate in discussions. If you have more people, you might want to break up the main group into smaller subgroups, and appoint facilitators for those subgroups. Encourage those who show up at the first meeting to commit to attending for the duration of the study, as this will help the group members get to know one another and create stability and community.

## Session Structure

Each session will follow the same basic structure, as follows:

### Opening Reflection

From the second lesson on, each session will begin with an opening time of reflection, when the group members will share what they learned or practiced since the last meeting. Depending on the amount of time you have, you can keep this discussion short and to the point or encourage deeper sharing.

### Session Introduction

Read aloud the introductory paragraph and the questions. They will help to get the group members thinking about the topic at hand. Some people may want to tell a long story in response to one of these questions, but the goal in this section is to keep the answers brief.

### Watch the Video

Watch the video together as a group. Encourage your group members to fill in the blanks in the study guide as they watch, so they can recall the main points later. Then read aloud the opening prayer.

### Icebreaker

The icebreaker activity or discussion is designed to lighten the mood and get participants engaged and talking.

### Group Discussion

During this time, the group will focus on learning and beginning to apply the biblical and spiritual principles underlying Ruth's practical insights. In many cases there will be no one "right" answer to the questions. Answers will vary, especially when the group members are being asked to share their personal experiences. The personal stories will make this material come alive and build friendships and community, so be sure to encourage sharing.

In this section, it's generally not a good idea to have everyone answer every question—a free-flowing discussion is more desirable. Be careful neither to let a discussion run on too long nor to cut off a productive discussion just to move to another question. Intervene gently to guide the pacing. End the discussion with the closing prayer.

### Personal Study

Each session contains three between-sessions activities called "Personal Study" that the group members should complete during the week. These activities will encourage them to spend time in God's Word and help them practice the concepts presented during the group session.

## Weekly Preparation

As the leader, here are a few things you should do to prepare for each meeting:

- *Read through the session*. This will help you to become familiar with the content and know how to structure the discussion times.
- *Decide which questions you want to discuss and familiarize yourself with them.* Based on the time you have available, you may not be able to get through all of the introductory, icebreaker, and group discussion questions, so choose those questions that you definitely want to cover.
- *Pray for your group.* Pray for your group members throughout the week and ask God to lead them as they study his Word.
- *Ready the room and the equipment.* Make sure the meeting room is arranged properly and any beverages or snacks are coordinated. Check that the video

player operates properly. Bring along extra pens, papers, and Bibles for those who may need them.

## Structuring the Session Time

You will need to determine with your group how long you want to meet each week so you can plan your time accordingly. Generally, most groups like to meet for either sixty minutes or ninety minutes, so you could use one of the following schedules:

| Section | 60 minutes | 90 minutes |
| --- | --- | --- |
| Opening Reflection | 5 minutes | 20 minutes |
| Session Introduction | 5 minutes | 10 minutes |
| Watch the Video | 15 minutes | 15 minutes |
| Icebreaker | 10 minutes | 15 minutes |
| Group Discussion | 25 minutes | 30 minutes |

In addition to the basic outline given above, we have also indicated approximate times in the session itself based on a sixty-minute session; you may adjust those times according to the time you've allotted. The time for watching the video itself will vary slightly from session to session but will take approximately fifteen to twenty minutes. As the group leader, it is up to you to keep track of the time and keep things moving along according to your schedule. If you would like to spend time enjoying refreshments or taking prayer requests, be sure to build that into your timing calculations as well.

## Group Dynamics

Leading a group through *Living Well Spending Less/Unstuffed* will prove to be highly rewarding both to you and your group members. However, this doesn't mean you will not encounter any challenges along the way! Discussions can get off track. Group members may not be sensitive to the needs and ideas of others. Some might worry they will be expected to talk about matters that make them feel awkward. Others may express comments that result in disagreements. To help ease this strain on you and the group, consider the following tips:

- When someone raises a question or comment that is off the main topic, suggest you deal with it another time, or, if you feel led to go in that direction, let the group know you will be spending some time discussing it.
- If someone asks a question you don't know how to answer, admit it and move on, or ask if someone else can help give an answer.
- Don't be concerned if the group members are quiet or slow to share. People are often quiet when they are pulling together their ideas. Just ask a question and let it hang in the air until someone shares. You can then say, "Thank you. What about others? What do you think?" Alternatively, you may move on to another question if you are unable to spark a helpful discussion.
- If you find one or two people are dominating the discussion time, direct a few questions to others in the group. Outside the main group time, ask the more dominating members to help you draw out the quieter ones. Work to make them a part of the solution instead of the problem.
- When a disagreement occurs, encourage the group members to process the matter in love. Encourage those on opposite sides to restate what they heard the other side say about the matter, and then invite each side to evaluate if that perception is accurate. Lead the group in examining other Scriptures related to the topic and look for common ground.

When any of these issues arise, encourage your group members to follow these words from the Bible: "Love one another" (John 13:34), "If it is possible, as far as it depends on you, live at peace with everyone" (Romans 12:18), and "Be quick to listen, slow to speak and slow to become angry" (James 1:19). This will make your group time more rewarding and beneficial for everyone who attends.

Thank you again for your willingness to lead your group. May God reward your efforts and dedication and make your time together fruitful for his kingdom.

# Living Well, Spending Less

## 12 Secrets of the Good Life

*Ruth Soukup*

Have you ever felt that your life—and budget—is spiraling out of control? Do you sometimes wish you could pull yourself together but wonder exactly how to manage all the scattered pieces of a chaotic life? Is it possible to find balance? In a word, yes! Ruth Soukup knows firsthand how stressful an unorganized life and budget can be. Through personal stories, biblical truth, and practical action plans, she will inspire you to make real and lasting changes to your personal goals, home, and finances. With honesty and the wisdom of someone who has been there, Ruth will help you:

- Discover your "sweet spot"—that place where your talents and abilities intersect.
- Take back your time and schedule by making simple shifts in your daily habits.
- Reduce stress in your home and family by clearing out the clutter.
- Stop busting your budget and learn to cut your grocery bill in half.

**What Others Are Saying:**

*"An incredible book that will teach you how to spend smart without compromising a great life. Ruth's stories and practical advice will make you want to be a better mother, wife, sister, and friend."*
—RACHEL CRUZE, coauthor with Dave Ramsey of *Smart Money Smart Kids*

*"Ruth knows firsthand how mamas like us live crazy busy lives, and she steps in as a friend to help us manage and love every minute of it. She offers her best tips for gaining control over the chaos with wisdom-based insights on all things thrifty and family. I'll be reading it again and again!"*
—RENEE SWOPE, bestselling author of *A Confident Heart*

*Available in stores and online!*

# Unstuffed

## Decluttering Your Home, Mind, & Soul

*Ruth Soukup*

STUFF. It's everywhere. Lurking in corners and closets, spilling onto counters and coffee tables, creating havoc everywhere we look. And it's not just the physical clutter that weighs us down. Oh no, it is the stress of overbooked schedules and the weight of life that sometimes feels oppressive and totally out of whack.

*New York Times* bestselling author Ruth Soukup feels your pain—she has been there too. Through personal stories, biblical truth, and practical action plans, she will inspire and empower each of us to finally declutter not just our home but our mind and soul as well.

In this book, together we will:

- Create a comprehensive vision for our homes and make instant changes to improve its overall function.
- Discover that more closet space is not the solution, and instead learn how to set strict limits for the stuff we bring in.
- Overcome the frustration of dealing with our kids' influx of stuff and implement practical solutions for keeping the chaos at bay.
- Recognize the pitfalls of an overstuffed schedule *before* it gets out of hand, and instead learn to combat the culture of busy that keeps us running from one thing to the next.
- Finally conquer that mountain of paperwork that threatens to tumble down around us at any moment.
- Let go of the guilt that gets attached to gifts and instead learn to separate our loved ones from their stuff.
- Begin to cultivate our real friendships while eliminating the toxic relationships that weigh us down.

*Available in stores and online!*